ZOË'S
SHEEP

by Rose Bursik

Henry Holt and Company

New York

"I'm not tired," Zoë told her father as he tucked her into bed one night.

"Try counting sheep," he said. "That will make you sleepy."

"Okay," said Zoë. She closed her eyes and began counting. But to her surprise...

Sheep number one liked to dance,

number two was fond of plants,

number three made quite a racket,

number four tried on a jacket,

number five was an acrobatic fellow,

number six's favorite color was yellow,

number seven enjoyed good books,

number eight gave rude looks,

number nine started a fray...

...but number ten saved the day!

Henry Holt and Company, Inc. / *Publishers since 1866*
115 West 18th Street, New York, New York 10011.
Henry Holt is a registered trademark of Henry Holt and Company, Inc.
Copyright © 1994 by Rose Bursik / All rights reserved.
Published in Canada by Fitzhenry & Whiteside, Ltd.,
195 Allstate Parkway, Markham, Ontario L3R 4T8.

Library of Congress Cataloging-in-Publication Data
Bursik, Rose.
Zoë's sheep / Rose Bursik.
Summary: When Zoë can't sleep, her father suggests counting sheep,
but her sheep like to create a ruckus.
[1. Counting. 2. Sheep—Fiction. 3. Bedtime—Fiction. 4. Stories in rhyme.] I. Title.

GAYLORD M